Mythology :

GREEK GODS

Myths, Legends

and

Ancient History

2nd Edition

by Roy Jackson

Table of Contents

Introduction

Haven't you always had a fascination for the different myths from different parts of the world? Do ancient beliefs fascinate you? If yes, then Greek mythology is something you should learn about – filled with tales of gods and goddesses, of heroes and monsters and mortals, it contains everything that a good book must have! One story about the Greek gods is all it takes for us to pay rapt attention to these stories. If you wanted to hear more about these, or simply wanted to reminisce about what you had heard when you were younger, this book is the one you need.

Greek mythology has contributed a lot to modern associations of art – the architecture, the stories, and the art stand as proof to that. However, in this eBook, we shall focus on the Greek gods, because there is so much that can be said about them – and so much to know!

This book tries to give you an idea of how the Greek gods were, and the stories that were most often associated with them – it also attempts to give you an idea of not only the main Greek gods, but also other deities such as the primordial deities and the Titans. This way, you will have a comprehensive idea of Greek mythology and Greek gods by the time you are finished.

Well, now it is time to start on your journey back in time – so you can witness how things were back then. What are you waiting for? Sit back, relax, and leaf through the pages as you get transported back to ancient Greece!

Enjoy your journey...

Chapter 1: Primordial Deities – Creation

The first mention of the primordial deities was observed in the Creation Myth, a complex tale that talks about how the Greek believe the world came into being. This has been best explained in the poem named Theogony, composed by Hesiod. The most important deities involved during Creation are mentioned below.

Chaos

According to Hesiod, Chaos was the first thing that ever was. It was the primordial state of existence from which the first deities appeared. The description of Chaos is not as confusion, but as a dark void of space, bottomless and endless in all directions. It is unclear if anything existed beyond this void, or whether the entire universe was itself the void – before Creation happened. It is from Chaos that Gaea, Tartarus, Erebus, Nyx, and Eros came to be.

Some people considered Chaos to be that vast and dark void out of which everything appeared. Some believe Eurynome, the goddess of everything, appeared from Chaos, and created the universe as we know it. Some others called it the womb of blackness out of which the Cosmic Egg appeared.

Gaea

In Greek mythology, Gaea personified the earth. To put it simply, she was Mother Earth. She emerged from Chaos along with four other deities, and was one of the first beings that came to be. She was responsible for the creation of the earth and the universe as we see it today. Sometimes she is seen as the earth and sometimes she is seen as the deity responsible for the creation of the entire universe. By herself, she was responsible for the creation of Uranus, the Sky full of stars, and Pontus, the deep of the Sea.

Through Pontus, she bore the deities of the sea: Phorcys, Thaumas, Nereus, and others. Through Uranus, another primordial deity, she bore many children. First, the twelve Titans were born: Oceanus, Coeus, Crius,

Theia, Rhea, Hyperion, Iapetus, Themis, Mnemosyne, Phoebe, Tethys, and Cronos. She then gave birth to the three Cyclopes (One-eyed giants): Brontes, Steropes, and Arges. Then came the three Hecatoncheires (Hundred Handed giants): Cottus, Briareus, and Gyges. Each of the Hecatoncheires had fifty heads.

Uranus was believed to be cruel and evil. He hid his children, the Hecatoncheires and the Cyclopes in Tartarus so they would never see light, and then delighted in this evil deed. Gaea was pained by this, and she asked her children, the Titans, to overthrow their lusty father. Cronos was the most daring and wily among them, and only he came forth to take the sickle that their mother had fashioned out of the earth. He then proceeded to castrate his father while his four brothers ambushed him and help him captive.

After the castration of Uranus, Gaea mated with Tartarus to give birth to Typhon and Echidna, the mother of monsters.

Tartarus

According to the Theogony, Tartarus was the third primordial deity, and the second to rise from Chaos, after Gaea. In Greek mythology, Tartarus was not only a deity, but also a place in the Underworld. The distance between earth and the place Tartarus was said to be the same as the distance between heaven and earth. A bronze anvil dropped from heaven would fall for nine days before reaching earth and would fall for nine more days before reaching Tartarus. The deity was said to guard over the place, which was often shown as incredibly dark and gloomy. The wicked were said to be tormented and made to suffer in this place.

Sometimes Tartarus was considered to be the same as Hades, or the Underworld. Many a times though, it was considered a deep, bottomless pit, used to jail and torment those who have committed the most horrible deeds. Cronos and the other Titans were sent to Tartarus after the victory of Olympians in the Titanomachy.

Aether

Aether or Ether was one of the primordial deities in Greek mythology, the elemental ones who were born first. He is also called Acmon, and his name means "light". Aether is the embodiment and elemental god of the glowing upper air of the heaven, also called the substance of light. It is said that the upper air that the gods breathe in heaven is purer than the normal air that the mortals breathe, and Aether embodies that air.

There are many theories of Creation, and all of them tell different origins of Aether. He was the child of Erebus and Nyx, according to Hesiod's Theogony, known as Zeus' wall of defense which locked Tartarus away from the rest of cosmos. Alcman claims Aether was the father of Ouranos (or the Sky), while Aristophanes states that he was a son of Erebus. In yet another account, Damascius considers him to be a sibling of Erebus and Chaos, who are all children of Chronos or Father Time.

According to yet another myth, in the beginning the universe was a cosmic egg. Time and Inevitability encircled it like serpents, and when they constricted it, the matter was squeezed with boundless force and two hemispheres were formed. After the atoms organized themselves, the lighter ones formed the Aether and Wind (Chaos), while the heavier ones formed the Earth (Gaea) and Ocean (Pontus).

Eros

Greek mythology makes references to two deities named Eros. However, the one who was present during creation is said to be the god associated with generations, and with establishing harmony among the world. Said to be a very beautiful primordial deity, Eros was responsible for procreation in the Universe. He was also the artistic urge of the nature, responsible for the coming into order of all things in the cosmos. He was also worshipped as Protogonus, the first-born.

Erebus

Erebus, or Erebos, is a primordial deity, one of the five who emerged out of Chaos, and is said to be the embodiment of darkness and shadows. While he does not occupy the centre stage in Greek mythology, he was the father to many deities through Nyx, his sister, some of them being Hemera, Hypnos, the Moirai, Styx, and Thanatos.

Erebus was also believed to be part of Hades or the Underworld, according to some later myths. When people died, their souls had to pass through a land of gloom and darkness immediately after, which was known as Erebus. The god Hades is also sometimes referred to as Erebus, although the literal meaning of Erebus is "darkness" only. It was called the dark place between the Earth and the Underworld. The landscape or the whole realm of the Underworld was also referred to as Erebus at times. It was believed to be a harsh and unforgiving land.

Nyx

Nyx is the Greek primordial goddess who personifies the

night. Like the others before her, she emerged Chaos – and it is said that she has great power within her. She is associated with being the mother of Hypnos (sleep), Thanatos (death), Nemesis (revenge), Eris (strife) and other deities who were personified as well. Through her brother and partner, Erebus, she bore two children – a son and a daughter. The son, Ether, represented the upper air, or heavenly light, while the daughter, Hemera, represented the day, or daylight.

It is said that Nyx's home is located in Tartarus, and that Hemera left the place while Nyx entered it, and Nyx left while Hemera entered – which served as an explanation for the cyclic day and night cycles observed. It is similar to the cooperative yet tense relationship between the Ratri (Night) and Usha (Day) mentioned in the Indian scripture Rig-Veda.

Pontus

Pontus is the ancient sea god, and was Gaea's son, as previously mentioned. Through Gaea, he was the father of the representations of the dangerous and strong aspects of the sea. Through Thalassa, a primordial sea goddess, he was the father of all life in the sea.

Uranus

Uranus was the primordial Greek god who personified the sky, or heaven. He was born of Gaea alone. Later, however, he (the sky) wrapped himself around Gaea (the earth) and through their union came forth the Cyclopes, Hecatoncheires, and the Titans.

Uranus hated the Hecatoncheires and imprisoned them – which angered Gaea. She conspired against him and decided to ask her son Cronos (the youngest of the Titans) to help her with it. She created a sickle for this purpose. As Gaea and Uranus lay together, Cronos castrated Uranus using the sickle. From the blood that spilled, the giants and ash-tree nymphs were created – and from his genitals, which were cast into the sea, came forth Aphrodite. After this castration, the sky stayed in its place during the nights, and did not cover the Earth, then (which serves as another explanation for the day and night cycles.

Chapter 2: Primordial Deities – The Titans

The Titans, as you can recall, were the sons and daughters of Gaea and Uranus. They are often referred to as the Twelve Titans – Coues, Crius, Cronos, Hyperion, Iapetus, and Oceanus were the sons, while Mnemosyne, Phoebe, Rhea, Tethys, Theia, and Themis were the daughters. These twelve form the first generation of the Titans. Their children are a part of the second generation of the Titans. This chapter focuses on the primordial deities, the Titans – and gives you an overview about them.

Cronos

Cronos might have been the youngest of the Titans, but he was still considered their leader – possibly because he was the most ambitious of the children of Uranus and Gaea. He is depicted carrying a sickle (the same one he used to castrate his father and overthrow him), which was used to harvest crops. Cronos was the Titan of the ages and time. It is also said that he ruled over earth during its Golden Age. His wife was Rhea, who was also his sister.

One of the most important tales surrounding Cronos has relations to how cruel he was. After he overthrew his father, there was a prophecy made concerning him, which stated that one of his children would be responsible for Cronos facing a fate much like his father's. Hence, Cronos decided to swallow his children whole every time Rhea gave birth – while it didn't kill them (because they were immortal), there was no way they could escape – this was the fate of three of his daughters and two of his sons.

Soon after, Rhea approached her mother so she could understand how to overthrow Cronos, saw the future, and made a plan. She secretly gave birth to another son, Zeus, and kept him hidden. Rhea gave Cronos a rock wrapped in a blanket instead, which Cronos did not suspect.

When Zeus finally grew up, he faced Cronos, and with the help of Gaea, forced him to regurgitate his children, which was the beginning of the Titanomachy as we know it, a ten year long war between the Titans and the gods. It was a war that was eventually won by the gods, after which Zeus ordered for most of the Titans to be imprisoned in the pits of Tartarus.

Coeus

He was regarded as the Titan god of intellect and inquisitiveness. The name Coeus means "questioning". Thus, he was associated with rational thinking. He was a son of Uranus and Gaea. He, and his brothers Crius, Hyperion, and Iapetus, were the four pillars that held the earth and the heavens apart, and they played an important part in the overthrowing of their father, Uranus, each of them holding him in place on one side. Coeus was the pillar in the North. Through his sister, Phoebe, he was the father of Asteria and Leto.

After the Titanomachy, when many of the Titans were banished to Tartarus, Coeus was the only one who managed to break his chains and try to escape. He was stopped and forced to stay by the guardian of the gates of the Underworld, the three-headed dog Cerberus.

Crius

Not only was he associated with the constellation, Aries,

the Titan was also the god who measured the year. This is because the rise of this constellation in the south marks the beginning of a New Greek year. He was, as you might have guessed, the pillar in the South. He married Eurybia, a daughter of Pontus, and together, they had three children, Astraeus, Pallas and Perses.

Iapetus

Another Titan associated with time, Iapetus was the Titan god of mortality, as well as that of violent death. Some myths also link him to craftsmanship. The fourth Titan holding the earth and the heavens apart, he was representative of the pillar in the West. His children and he are said to be the ancestors of mankind, and this has been explained in how they derived some of their worst qualities from his sons. He married the daughter of Oceanus, Asia, and had four sons. Atlas gave humanity excessive daring, Prometheus bequeathed treachery and scheming, Epimetheus gave stupidity, and Menoetius passed down violence.

Hyperion

The name 'Hyperion' is said to come from a term that means "the watcher from above". He was the Titan god of light – and by extension, he was also considered the father of the lights of heaven. He was the Titan deity who symbolized wisdom and watchfulness. Among his four brothers who held the earth and heaven apart, he was the pillar in the East. His sister, Theia, was his wife. They had three children together: Helios (the Sun), Eos (the Dawn), and Selene (the Moon). Hyperion was a powerful Titan, but he is not mentioned in the Titanomachy.

Oceanus

Oceanus was the oldest son of Uranus and Gaea. According to the ancient Greeks, a river named Okeanos encircled all of Earth – and Oceanus was the Titan god of this river. Some believe that he was the god of the largest bodies of water known by the Greeks. Tethys was his wife and his sister – their children were called the Oceanids, who were gods of smaller bodies of water, such as rivers and springs. He did not participate in the Titanomachy, and thus, Zeus let him continue ruling his kingdom.

Rhea

Rhea was the sister and wife of the Titan, Cronos. The name Rhea translates to "that which flows". Her conspiring against him was the main reason he was overthrown by his son, Zeus. Cronos' and Rhea's other children together were Hades, Poseidon, Demeter,

Hestia, and Hera. She had hidden Zeus from Cronos in Crete. Owing to this reason, a temple stands in the place for her worship. Rhea, although regarded as the "mother of gods", never had a strong cult like Gaea did. In art, her features were indistinguishable from Cybele.

Phoebe

Phoebe was the Titan goddess associated with wisdom and thoughtfulness. Apart from this, she is also referred to as the Titan of prophecy, because of her association with the oracle of Delphi. She was married to her brother, Coeus, through whom she had two daughters, Asteria and Leto. It is because of their grandmother's name that the names of the twin Olympians Apollo and Artemis became synonymous with Phoebe and Phoebus. She did not participate in the Titanomachy, and hence, she was not condemned like the other Titans.

Tethys

While her husband, Oceanus, was associated with larger bodies of water, Tethys was the Titan goddess of fresh water sources. Her children with Oceanus included not only the various river gods, but also the water nymphs and Nephelai (clouds).

Some stories also call her the nurse. This may be

because she took care of Hera during the Titanomachy, at Rhea's request. Another interesting story concerning Tethys is associated with Hera's displeasure with the position of the constellations Ursa Major and Ursa Minor – Tethys caused them to be such that they never dipped below the horizon, which indicates that her powers were very great.

Mnemosyne

She was the Titan goddess of memory. The nine Muses were born as a result of her union with Zeus – it is said that this happened because Zeus slept with Mnemosyne for nine consecutive days. Owing to her own ability, and that of the Muses, she is also associated with languages and words.

Theia

Theia was the Titan goddess of sight. This may be because of the fact that her children with Hyperion were the personifications of the Sun, Moon and Dawn, all of which are associated with sight. She was also associated with glittering gemstones and metals – and sometimes with the idea of glory by itself.

Themis

Themis served as a representation of order. She was the Titan goddess of natural order, moral order, and divine law. She was the second wife that Zeus had – and through their union, bore six children, who were later associated with order in time, and justice. She was earlier worshipped as the Oracle of Delphi.

Through one of her children, Hores, she performed the duty of natural order, making sure time could not be stopped. Through Deke, Erene, Eunomia and Moires, she performed her role with regard to moral justice. Apart from this, she performed her prophetic role through Astraea, and with the help of nymphs.

Second Generation Titans

Next, we move on to the second generation of Titans. Some of these participated in the Titanomachy as well – but other had some other interesting roles and personifications to play.

Asteria

Asteria was the daughter of Coeus and Phoebe. Through the Titan, Perses, she was the mother of Hecate. She is considered the Titan goddess of falling stars and nocturnal oracles. To escape from Zeus and his advances, she turned into a quail – and eventually became the quail island of Ortygia. Later, this island was recognized as the Delos, the floating island where Asteria's sister, Leto found refuge when she was being pursued by Hera.

Leto

Leto was the sister of Asteria, and is known for being the mother of the twin Olympians, Apollo and Artemis. The story around their birth is a dramatic one. Leto was pregnant with the twins through Zeus, and this angered Hera, as she was Zeus' wife. Thus, she made sure all the lands shunned Leto. Leto then went in search of a place that would accept her – and found the floating island of Delos. As it was not tied down, it was not technically considered land. There, she gave birth to the twins secretly.

Astraeus

Astraeus, also known as Astraios, was another second generation Titan, and was the son of Crius and Eurybia. He was the Titan god of the dusk and the winds – thus, it only seemed perfect that he married Eos, the Titan goddess of the dawn. They had many children together –

the most notable being the four Anemoi, who were wind deities, and the Astra Planeta, who represented the planets, Saturn, Jupiter, Mars, Venus, and Mercury.

Pallas

Pallas was the son of the Titans Eurybia and Crius, and the brother of Astraeus and Perses. He was the Titan god of war craft. Through his wife, Styx, he fathered many children – like Nike, Bia and Kratos. He was killed by Athena during the Titanomachy.

Perses

Perses was the Titan god of destruction, and was born to Crius and Eurybia. He was the father of the Hecate, the goddess of magic and witchcraft.

Atlas

Atlas was a second generation Titan, and was the son to Iapetus and Clymene. He had three brothers: Prometheus, Epimetheus, and Menoetius. Atlas was the Titan of navigation and astronomy. He and his brother Menoetius sided with the Titans during the Titanomachy, while Prometheus and Epimetheus sided with the Olympians. It is said that Atlas was the one who lead the Titans in the war, and this is why he is also referred to as "The General" sometimes. After the Titans lost the war, Atlas' punishment was also very severe. Zeus condemned him to hold up the sky (Uranus, the father of Titans) forever on his shoulders, so as to prevent the reunion of Gaea and Uranus. Atlas is often depicted as holding up the Earth on his shoulders, but that is a misconception. He also came to be associated with celestial spheres and the globe.

Atlas was married to Phoebe, another Titan, with whom he fathered many children, such as the Hesperides, the Hyas, Calypso, and Maera. There are several later myths associated with Atlas. One of them is of Perseus, when he went to northwest Africa. Atlas, a giant, tried to drive him away, but Perseus turned him to stone with the head of Medusa whom he had already slayed. It is said that the Atlas Mountains are the petrified giant Atlas himself. Another story from the Twelve Labors of Heracles tells of how Heracles asked for Atlas' help when he had to fetch the golden apple from the garden of the Hesperides, protected by the dragon Ladon. Atlas tried to trick Heracles into holding up the sky for him forever, but the latter managed to escape with the apples.

Prometheus

Prometheus is one of the brothers of Atlas, and he symbolized foresight, or forethought. It was because of this reason that he sided with the Olympians during the Titanomachy, and hence was not condemned like the other Titans.

However, the story of Prometheus does not end here. He was regarded as the protector of human beings. Thus, when Zeus hid fire from all human beings, it was Prometheus who stole it back for them. His actions angered Zeus, who tied down the Titan to a rock, where an eagle would peck and eat at his liver every day. During the nights, the liver would regenerate, and the eagle would return the next day. This cycle of torment continued till Heracles freed Prometheus by slaying the eagle.

Prometheus was one of the second generation Titans, a son of the Titans Iapetus and Clymene (an Oceanid). He was brother to Epimetheus, Atlas and Menoetius. The name Prometheus derives from the Greek word meaning 'forethought'. Hence, Prometheus was the Titan god of forethought and foresight. It was because of this reason that he sided with the Olympians during the Titanomachy, helping the Olympians overthrow the Titans. After their victory, he was not banished to Tartarus like many other Titans for this reason.

Prometheus was always presented as a guardian and benefactor of mankind. In the myth of the Trick at

Mecone, Prometheus presented a choice to the king of the gods, Zeus. He asked Zeus to choose between beef hidden inside an ox's stomach and bones wrapped in fat. The former represented something pleasing hidden inside a repulsive exterior, while the latter represented something inedible hidden inside an attractive exterior. Zeus made the mistake of choosing the latter, and this set a precedent for what humans would sacrifice to the gods. So the humans started keeping the meat for themselves and sacrificed the bones to their gods.

Zeus was enraged by this trickery, and as a punishment on the mortals, he decided to hide "fire" away from them, but Prometheus, still being benevolent to humanity, stole the fire and gave it back to humans. Zeus' anger knew no limits, and he asked the god Hephaestus to create the first woman, Pandora. The myth of Pandora tells about how she was too curious for her own good, and opened a box, called the Pandora's Box, and let out all sorts of evil into the mortal world.

Zeus also tied down Prometheus to a rock, where an eagle would peck and eat at his liver every day. During the nights, the liver would regenerate because of his immortality, and the eagle would return the next day to eat it again. This cycle of torment continued till the demigod Heracles freed Prometheus by slaying the eagle.

Epimetheus

While his brother was associated with foresight, Epimetheus was associated with hindsight – and thus, was represented as being foolish. This is observed in one of the tales surrounding him. He and Prometheus were responsible for distributing traits to all animals – as Epimetheus lacked foresight, he did not have a positive trait left to give humans. It is also said that Epimetheus accepted Pandora, as a gift from the gods.

Styx

Styx was a daughter of the Titans Tethys and Oceanus, thus receiving the title of an Oceanid. She was the deity of the ancient river Styx which flows through the underworld. Being married to Pallas, she gave birth to four children: Kratos, Nike, Zelus, and Bia. She didn't support the Titans during the Titanomachy. Instead, she fought on the side of the Olympians, and after their victory, Zeus honored her by giving her name to the binding oath the gods took.

It is said that the river Styx acted as a boundary between the mortal world and the underworld. The river was sometimes believed to carry lost hopes and dreams of the dead. A popular legend around the river is that of Achilles. When Achilles was just a little baby, his mother dipped him in Styx, holding him by his heel. This made him invulnerable, except in his heel with which his mother had held him. This myth is also where the term "Achilles' heel", meaning "a weak spot", comes from.

Menoetius

Menoetius is one of the brothers of Atlas. He is described as being very proud, even at the end, which was one of his many downfalls. He was banished to Tartarus after the Titanomachy. He was the Titan god of rash behavior and violent anger.

Eos

Eos was the daughter of Hyperion and Theia, and is the Titan goddess of the dawn. Every morning, she rose from her home, spreading light till the heavens. It is also said that her tears are responsible for the dew we see in the mornings.

Helios

Helios was the Titan god of the Sun. While some people relate him to Apollo, it must be noted that the two are two separate deities, and not the same person. He drove the chariot of the sun every day- in the morning, across the sky, and in the night, reached the East again through

Oceanus. The horses that Helios is the charioteer of are said to be made of fire.

Selene

Selene was the Titan goddess of the moon, and the sister to Helios and Eos. Like her brother Helios, she too drives a chariot across the heavens – but hers is referred to as the moon chariot. Comparisons are drawn between her and the Olympian Athena, but the two are distinctly different – and Selene is the only goddess recognized as personifying the moon.

Chapter 3: Introduction to Olympian Gods and Goddesses

The focus of the next two chapters will be the Olympian gods (sometimes referred to just as the Olympians), who were considered the most important deities in the Greek pantheon. While this chapter gives you a general overview about them, the next one focuses on the specific stories surrounding them.

It is believed that the Olympian gods had their abode on Mount Olympus, where they resided – which gave them their name. Another important factor associated with the Olympians is that there were twelve of them. However, different sources of Greek mythology vary on who they believe was the twelfth Olympian – Dionysus or Hestia.

While we may not have an answer to that question ourselves, in this chapter, we provide you with a comprehensive list of those Greek gods and goddesses who were considered an Olympian by any source, not just a specific one. Thus, the list provided below has more than twelve gods.

Zeus

Zeus, also known as Jupiter in his Roman form, was the Greek god of sky and the king of Olympian gods. He was the son of Cronos and Rhea. Despite being the youngest Olympian to be born, he is mentioned first on this list because he was responsible for overthrowing his cruel father, the Titan Cronos. Thus, he is widely regarded as the leader of not only the Olympians, but also the mortals – as he ruled over them. Zeus is famously associated with his weapon, the lightning bolt, which he threw at those who defied his will or irked him. He especially loathed liars and vow breakers. He was married to Hera, but also had numerous affairs with other people – which served as the main reason for the several differences between the two. Zeus is father to many Olympians, including Ares and Athena among others.

Zeus was the governing deity of the cosmos, known as the king of the skies, and was considered by the ancient Greeks as the god of all natural occurrences in the sky. He was regarded as the embodiment of the laws of nature and the father of immortals and mortal men alike. He used his shield, the Aegis, to create various natural phenomena of the sky and the air, like intense darkness, storms, and tempests. He had lightning and thunder at his command, which could wreak havoc if he gave the word. He could also make it rain, rejuvenating the earth with water.

Zeus represented the grand and unchanging laws of the harmonious order, being the epitome of natural operations. In contrast to what his father stood for – absolute time or eternity – Zeus was the god of structured and controlled time, like the change of seasons and the chain of day and night after each other. He stood for the laws of nature which governed both the physical and spiritual world. He also governed the deities of Olympus and saw to it that they performed their duties properly, punishing their transgressions and settling disputes between them.

He was often regarded as a benevolent ruler and father of mortal men, taking a paternal interest in their deeds, and looking after their well-being as a father would. He was always attentive to the mortal world, which he created himself, rewarding virtuous qualities like charity and fairness, while punishing the negative traits like cruelty. As a king, he took special interest in princes and kingdoms, providing valuable counsel. He was regarded as the source of royal power and the protector of society.

Hera

Hera, known as Juno in her Roman form, was the wife and sister of Zeus, and most often considered the queen of the gods. Known as the supreme goddess, she was also the patron of marriage and childbirth, even though her relationship with her own partner was filled with distress. She had an exceptional interest in protecting womenfolk, especially the married ones. The cow and peacock were sacred to Hera, and the city of Argos held a special place in her heart.

Although mostly known to be a fair and just goddess, she didn't extend her justness to the women whom Zeus had affairs with. She had a knack of interfering with the lives of the mortals romantically involved with her husband and the children who were thus born from such unions, altering the course of their lives and trying to harm them in various ways. Heracles is a prime example of this nature of Hera. She had three children with Zeus – Ares, the god of war, Hebe, the goddess of eternal youth, and Eileithyia, the goddess of childbirth. Apart from this, she was also the only parent of Hephaestus.

The relationship between Hera and her husband was a turbulent one. It even started out with trickery. It is said that initially, Zeus tried to sway Hera, but after countless failed attempts, he resorted to deceit. Taking the form of a sick cuckoo, he appeared before Hera, who took pity on the bird and held it close to her bosom to keep it warm. He then took his original form and raped Hera, taking advantage of her shock. She had to marry him to cover her shame.

Most of the stories in folklore concerning Hera are about her jealousy towards her husband's affairs and her plans for vengeance. In one notable incident, she took advantage of the way Zeus sometimes mistreated other gods, and convinced them to join her in a revolt against Zeus. She drugged her husband, and the others tied him to a couch. What happened next was unfortunately not in her favor, as all the gods began to argue over what to do next, and Briareus the Hecatoncheires (Hundred Handed One), who happened to be overhearing their arguments, stealthily untied Zeus' knots and freed him, for he was still grateful to Zeus for the kindness he had shown by freeing the Hecatoncheires during the Titanomachy. Zeus immediately got up and grabbed his thunderbolt, making all the other gods beg for his mercy. He then went on to punish Hera for her insolence, hanging her from the sky with chains. He freed Hera the next morning on the condition that she would never rebel against him again, which she agreed to as she had but little choice. This made her even bitterer, and while she never openly rebelled again, she interfered with her husband's plans many times, and outwit him at many instances.

Poseidon

Poseidon, known as Neptune in his Roman form, is considered one of the most important Olympians, along with Zeus and Hades. Together, they form the Trinity or the Big Three of the Greek mythology. They often appear together in stories and seem to have a troublesome relationship with each other, owing to their pride and greed. After overthrowing their father, Cronos, the three of them drew lots to decide who would get what share of the universe. He was made the lord of the sea, and the guardian of all things aquatic. He was father to Pegasus and the other horses. While married to a granddaughter of the Titan Oceanus, named Amphitrite, he had numerous affairs with other goddesses, and with mortals, much like his brother Zeus. He sired many demigod heroes, some of them really famous in the legends.

A story about his desire for Demeter tells how he created the first horse. Demeter had asked him to create the most beautiful animal in the world, as a way to deter him, and in an attempt to do so, he made the horse. Some other accounts say that he failed in his early attempts, creating many other animals instead, and by the time he created the horse, his desire for Demeter had decreased. He was considered the father of the Pegasus and other horses, and it is said that some of his demigod children could even talk to horses. The main protagonist in "Percy Jackson and the Olympians" (a popular children's book series written around Greek mythology) can talk to horses, Pegasi, and most aquatic creatures.

The trident was to Poseidon what the thunderbolt was to Zeus. Forged in the famous underwater forges by the Cyclopes, it was his weapon of choice. He could make the earth shake with the help of his trident, thus receiving the title of "earthshaker". In power, he was considered second only to the king of gods himself, the mighty Zeus. His trident could shatter any object.

He was believed to have a very greedy and difficult personality. Every so often, he would have a dispute with some other god or goddess, trying to take over the towns they were patrons of. His contest with Athena for the patronage of Athens is very famous.

Hades

Hades, known as Pluto to the Romans, was one of the Big Three Olympians. The other two were Zeus and Poseidon. After the three of them drew lots to decide who will get to rule what realm, Hades got the Underworld. This resulted in him becoming the lord of the Underworld and hence, the dead. However, he was not considered death himself. That role was for Thanatos, the young god of death. Some people don't consider Hades a true Olympian as he doesn't have a proper throne on Mount Olympus, and he seldom left his kingdom, some of the exceptions being the Winter Solstice and the Summer Solstice. His most famous weapon was the Helm of Darkness, which he donned to become invisible.

Hades was not liked much by the Greeks, and they avoided saying his name, for they feared some tragedy would befall them if they did and they would die sooner. So they gave Hades another name, "Plouton", which was derived from the Greek word for wealth. Since, all precious metals and minerals are extracted from the earth; he came to be known as the god of wealth as well. He was greedy, like his brother Poseidon, and wanted to expand his kingdom as much as possible. This is why he favored those people the acts of whom resulted in deaths. The Furies were welcome guests in his realm.

Demeter

Demeter was the Greek goddess of agriculture and fertility, and is associated with corn, grain, and the harvest. She is also known as Ceres to the Romans, which is where the word "cereals" comes from. It is believed that she provided nutrition to everyone on earth, and helped man by introducing him to wheat. Mortals in ancient times believed that praying to her would help their crops grow stronger. So they offered the first loaf of bread made from the yield of the year to Demeter. Livestock and agricultural products are sacred to her.

Demeter was also closely associated with seasonal change. She was the mother of Persephone through Zeus. Hades desired Persephone and abducted her to be his wife in the netherworld. Demeter, angered by her daughter's loss, took away all her gifts from humanity, causing plants to die and the land to become barren. This alarmed Zeus, and he asked Hades to return Persephone to her mother, but Hades made sure she had dined with him in the Underworld, and because she had eaten a pomegranate from his garden, she was bound to spend one-third of the year in the Underworld.

It is said that during these four months every year, Demeter grieves her daughter's absence, and creates winter by taking away her gifts. When Persephone returns, so does spring.

Athena

Athena, sometimes referred to as Athene, is the Greek goddess of wisdom, skill, reason, intelligent thought, arts and literature. In her Roman form, she is called Minerva. The myth surrounding her birth is that she sprang forth from the forehead of Zeus, as a product of thought, and that she was fully grown and armored as she burst out of his forehead. Some say that Zeus had a massive headache and he had to get his head cleaved open. This resulted in Athena's birth, and she is unique in that she had no mother.

Athena was also a maiden goddess and a very famous warrior, known for her meticulous war planning and ability to think on her feet. She specialized in war strategies. She was known to provide assistance to many Greek heroes during their quests, Odysseus and Jason being a few of those heroes. She taught many useful survival skills to mankind such as weaving, agriculture, and much more. She also invented devices such as the plow, the trumpet, the pot, the flute, the ship, and the chariot.

Athena was valiant and fierce in battle, but she only participated in those wars in which the defense of a state from outside enemies was at stake. She was the epitome of reason and purity. Being the favorite child of Zeus, she was permitted to use his weapons such as his shield Aegis. In fact, the Aegis is an important part of Athena's battle equipment, and she was always seen using it, striking the hearts of enemies with deadly fear. She was even allowed to use Zeus' thunderbolt according to some myths. The olive was her holy tree and the owl her sacred bird. The owl was often used to symbolize Athena.

The rivalry between Athena and Poseidon was famous. They competed to be the patron deity of the city of Athens, and Athena won after giving the Athenians an olive tree. That is when the city was named after her. Athena's weaving contest with the maiden Arachne is also a popular legend. Athena was challenged by Arachne, and after she won, she turned Arachne into a spider. This is where the term "arachnid" comes from. It is believed that all spiders are descendants of Arachne, and that they all hate Athena.

Apollo

Apollo was one of the twins born to the Titan Leto. The other one was his sister Artemis. Both of them were fathered by the king of the Olympians, Zeus. They are known as Archer Gods, shooting arrows nimbly from their godly bows. He was known as Phoebus, too. His holy tree was the laurel and his holy animal was the dolphin, although he was also known for his holy red cows.

Apollo was primarily the god of the Sun, and his most important task was to ride his four-horse chariot in the sky to move the Sun around the world. He was also the god of music; often seen playing his golden lyre which Hermes gifted him. Apollo gave humans the medical sciences and hence, was also called the god of medicine and healing. He was also regarded as the god of truth and of light. Apollo was famous for his poetry, and hence was also considered the god of poetry and verses. The Oracle of Delphi, sacred to Apollo, was said to utter prophecies in verses. Apollo was a handsome god and was considered the perfection of male beauty.

When Leto was pregnant with Apollo and Artemis, Hera got to know about her husband's infidelity, and cursed Leto so she wouldn't be able to give birth on land. Leto took refuge in a newly formed island, Delos, which was not considered a part of the land yet. Leto then gave birth to Artemis who, along with other inhabitants of the island, helped her in delivering Apollo. This was why Leto blessed them with favor of Apollo.

Apollo had gained the gift of prophecy by killing the deity Python, a son of Gaea, and he was worshipped as the prophetic deity in Delphi, where he had an Oracle. The Oracle of Delphi was really famous and people from all over the world visited it to know more about their future through Apollo's priestess Pythia. He was also worshipped in his birthplace, the island of Delos. These were the two major cults of Apollo.

As mentioned before, Apollo was also regarded as the god of healing and medicine. This could've been because of his own abilities, or through his son Asclepius. Either way, he was believed to bring health and salvation, although his arrows could bring disease and plague, too.

Apollo's duel with the wild god Pan is famous. Pan was the god of rustic music, and was really good at playing his reed pipes and Syrinx. The myth tells of Pan's challenge to Apollo, the former claiming to be a better musician than the latter. They competed to see who was a better musician, Apollo playing his golden lyre and Pan playing his reed pipes. In one account, everyone except Midas agreed that Apollo was better, and so he was to keep his title as the god of music. In another account, however, Apollo and Pan tied. Apollo then proceeded to declare that the one who would play his instrument upside down with more skill would win. Apollo had no problem in playing his lyre upside down, but Pan couldn't play his pipes upside down, and lost to the Sun god.

Artemis

Artemis, known as Diana in her Roman form, was a maiden goddess and the twin of Apollo. She and her twin brother are the children of Zeus and Leto (a Titan). After being hunted by Hera, Leto had finally found shelter at the island of Delos (also called Ortygia), where she gave birth to the twins. It is said that as soon as Artemis took birth, she started helping her mother as a midwife and delivered Apollo. This led her to believe that it was her fate to be a midwife and she would stay an eternal maiden. She became the protector of childbirth.

Considered as a counterpart to her brother, Apollo, she was the goddess of the moon, much as Apollo was the god of the sun, and rode a moon chariot. She took vows to stay an eternal virgin, and asked Zeus to bless her with eternal chastity, so she would never give in to potential lovers. She devoted herself to nature and hunting, and hence, became the goddess of virginity, the moon, the hunt, and natural environment. She protected the nature, the animals, and agriculture, too. Her weapon of choice is bow and arrow.

According to some legends, Artemis is known to travel with a pack of female warriors, known as the Hunters of Artemis. These are usually young girls who have vowed to remain maidens forever, pledging their allegiance to the goddess of chastity. The Hunters gain heightened senses and battle reflexes in exchange for their loyalty to the sisterhood, and they cannot die unless killed in battle. The Hunters are known to be very skilled warriors, and their preferable weapon is a bow and arrow, much like their patron.

Although she was famous for her vows of eternal maidenhood and she never gave in to romantic love, she was lovely lass, and had many suitors. There are many myths surrounding her. In the story of Actaeon, a hunting companion of Artemis, he sees her naked while she is bathing in a spring, and as a punishment, she transforms him into a stag that is mauled to death by his own hunting dogs. Some versions say he tried to rape her. Another popular story is that of Orion, who was considered to be the only person to ever win her heart. They were also hunting companions, and Artemis was awed by Orion's archery skills. The myths say that he was either killed accidently killed by Artemis herself, or by a scorpion which Gaea had sent.

Hestia

With her symbol appropriately being the hearth, Hestia was the maiden goddess of home, hearth, domestic life, and chastity. She was the oldest child of Cronos and Rhea. Zeus often made sure that she was safe from her suitors, as she too, had taken a vow of chastity. As Hestia presided over domestic life, she was worshipped by the household. But she was not publicly worshipped, as suggested by the lack of her shrines and temples. She was known for her kind and forgiving nature.

Hestia's Roman form was called Vesta, and contrary to the Greeks, she was actually publicly worshipped. She not only stood for domestic hearth, but also the public one. Initially, Hestia was a part of the Olympians, but she was later replaced to make place for the new god Dionysus. Poseidon and Apollo desired her, but she always declined, staying true to her vows of chastity. She was almost raped by a lesser god, Priapus, once, but the braying of a donkey saved her.

Aphrodite

Aphrodite was the goddess of love, sexual desire and beauty (especially female beauty). It is believed that Aphrodite was so beautiful that no man could escape her charms. She also had a magical girdle that made anyone who set eyes on her desire her. She was also considered the goddess of sex and attraction. She was married to Hephaestus, the god of craftsmen, but she had numerous affairs with other gods and mortals, most notably Ares. Among Romans, she was known as Venus.

There are two stories of her birth. According to one account, she was the daughter of Dione and Zeus. The more popular one, however, is the account in which she arose from the sea after Cronos, the Titan lord, castrated his father Uranus and tossed his genitals into the sea. She is also known as Cytherea as she was born on the island of Cythera in one story.

Hephaestus

Hephaestus, also known as Vulcan in his Roman form, was the Greek god sculptors, blacksmiths, craftsmen, and artisans. He was known for his inventions. He was also considered the god of metallurgy, fire and volcanoes. For this reason, he is sometimes depicted with a hammer, an anvil and a pair of blacksmith's pincers. According to Homer, he was a son of Zeus and Hera. However, Hesiod claims that Hera bore Hephaestus alone.

Hephaestus was a crippled god, and there are different myths regarding this in the Greek mythology. According to one version, Hephaestus was born so ugly that his mother, Hera, couldn't stand to look at him, and so she threw him from Mount Olympus. He was thus crippled, and raised in the ocean by Thetis and Eurynome. Some versions say he was raised by Nereids. Another story says that he tried to defend his mother from Zeus' advances, and the angry ruler of the gods threw him down from Olympus, causing his physical disability. It is said that he fell on Lemnos, an island, where he learned to be a master craftsman. Later, he was accepted back to Mount Olympus and given a throne, being appointed as the chief craftsman of the gods. He created magnificent shields, weapons, and armor for them.

Hephaestus was the husband of Aphrodite, and when he learned of her affair with Ares, the god of war, he decided to take revenge by devising a clever plan to humiliate them both in front of other Olympians.

Ares

In Greek mythology, Ares was the god of war. While the goddesses Enyo and Athena have also been closely associated with war, Ares signified a rawer side of wartime – the violence and untamed acts – as opposed to his sister Athena, the wisdom goddess, who symbolized tactical stratagem and military planning. He was known as Mars to the Romans.

Ares was the son of Zeus and Hera, and was detested by

both his parents. He was depicted as a violent personality, always inclined towards war and fighting, which often resulted in his defeat and subsequent humiliation. Homer's Iliad mentions that his father, Zeus, despised him more than anyone else. He had numerous affairs with his sister, Aphrodite, who was Hephaestus' wife. When Hephaestus found out about their affair, he was outraged, and he devised a clever plan which resulted in the mortification of both Ares and Aphrodite. Ares had many children with Aphrodite, including Eros (also known as Cupid), the infant god who is known to shoot people with his arrows and make them fall in love.

Ares had a few temple dedicated to him in ancient Greece, where armies would offer sacrifices to him for victory in war. Ares was respected among the warring tribes. The Spartans prayed to Enyalius who is sometimes seen as a son of Ares and sometimes as another form of Ares. Ares also had two other children with Aphrodite, Deimos (terror) and Phobos (fear), who always accompanied him when he went to war. Eris, the goddess of discord and strife, also accompanied him in his chariot.

Hermes

Hermes was the Greek god of commerce, travel, trade,

sports, boundaries, and communication. He was the son of Zeus and a nymph named Maia. He was known to be very quick and clever, being able to travel swiftly between different worlds. For this reason, he was appointed as the messenger of the gods, relaying messages between the mortal world and the world of gods. He also served as a guide to the souls of the dead, leading them to the underworld and their afterlife. It is said that Hermes traveled so fast with his iconic winged sandals.

Hermes was also the guardian and patron god of thieves, travelers and athletes. He was known to be very cunning and mischievous, occasionally playing tricks on other gods. It was either done to protect humans or for his own amusement. Hermes has a magical staff on which two intertwined serpents live. It has long been a symbol of trade and commerce.

Legend has it that when Hermes was born, he sneaked out of his crib and stole Apollo's holy cattle. He then sneaked back to his crib and acted innocent. When Apollo figured this out, he grabbed Hermes and took him to Zeus to complain about the thievery, but to his dismay, Zeus was only amused, and he didn't reprimand Hermes. Hermes felt bad for Apollo and, as a way to apologize, gave him the lyre which he had just invented. This is the same lyre Apollo is often depicted with in various paintings and artworks.

Hermes has been a recurring figure in folklore. In the Odyssey, Hermes was the one who instructed Odysseus to chew a magic herb which would make him invulnerable to Circe's transformation magic. Circe was a powerful witch who hated men and transformed those men who wandered to her island into pigs and other animals. In the story of Pandora, the first woman, Hermes was also the one who gave Pandora the ability to lie and to entice men with her words.

Dionysus

The youngest of the Olympians, Dionysus was not initially acknowledged as a god because he was a demigod son of Zeus through a mortal princess named Semele. However, some versions of Greek mythology identify him as an Olympian with a semi-god status. He discovered wine, and hence became the god of wine, winemaking, festivities, religious ecstasy, and theatre. He was also associated with insanity. The animals sacred to him were the panther and the tiger, and he was often depicted in artworks as a short round-bellied man wearing tiger skin. His Roman form is called Bacchus.

Chapter 4: Stories Involving the Olympians

Zeus and Hera

One of the stories that indicated the strained nature of the relationship between Zeus and Hera is as follows. While Zeus had tried to court Hera many times, he had remained unsuccessful. Thus, he took the form of a hurt cuckoo that Hera promptly felt sorry for and held close to her. This was when Zeus regained his true form and took advantage of the situation.

Other stories involving Zeus and Hera include her hatred for Heracles – who was the half mortal hero, a son of Zeus through one of his several affairs. This made Hera the step mother of Heracles. Not only did she try to kill

Heracles during his infancy, by sending snakes to the place where he was sleeping, but she also tried to make sure he wouldn't be able to complete the twelve labors (now famously known as the Twelve Labors of Heracles, because eventually, he did indeed complete them).

Zeus, Hera and Dionysus

The story involving Dionysus' birth is very interesting. Like it was mentioned previously, Semele was a mortal princess, and Hera often interfered with mortal lives when it concerned her relationship with Zeus. When Hera visited earth disguised as a crone, and discovered that the father of the child was indeed Zeus, she made Semele doubt Zeus – and his godly nature.

This ploy worked, as Semele asked Zeus to reveal himself in his true godly form. Despite various protests from him, she did not listen – and he finally obliged. However, mortals were never had the ability to see the true form of gods and live, and thus, Semele burned. In order to save the infant who was yet to be born, Zeus sewed him onto his thigh. Thus, Dionysus was born from Zeus' thigh – and this is the reason his name might mean twice born. Dionysus was widely revered in ancient Greece because of the same reason.

Poseidon and Demeter

One of the myths concerning Poseidon says that he pursued Demeter, who kept rejecting him. Eventually, she turned into a mare so she could hide from him, amongst other horses. However, he saw through that and caught her after turning into a stallion himself. The child that was born of this union was not human at all – but a horse that could talk in the manner humans do, by the name of Arion.

Poseidon and Athena

The relationship between Poseidon and Athena was a strained one, as the two often stood on opposing sides. Two instances of this can be observed in the famous stories surrounding them.

Medusa, unlike her two sister Gorgons, was a beautiful priestess at a temple dedicated to Athena. However, Poseidon refused to take Athena's vow of chastity seriously, and upon deciding that he liked Medusa, enticed the priestess and had sex with her in the temple. When Athena discovered this, she punished Medusa by making her like her sisters – her hair turned into snakes, and her gaze would result in turning people into stone. It is also said that Athena eventually guided the hero Perseus, as he went forth to slay Medusa.

One of the myths concerning Athens is the one about its naming – where Poseidon and Athena competed against each other to become the patron deity of the city. They were each to give the city folk one gift – from which the people would choose who they preferred. Poseidon sprung up a salt water spring, which gave the people a manner through which they could trade, but the water could not be consumed. Athena offered the first olive tree, which brought with it not only food, but wood and oil as well. The people accepted the olive tree – and thus, Athena became the patron goddess, and the city was named Athens.

Hades, Demeter, and Persephone

Persephone was the daughter of Demeter, and had been abducted against her wishes by Hades, who took her with him to the Underworld. In anger, Demeter cursed the lands such that there was no food available – which would have eventually wiped out mankind. She did not change her mind even after all the gods requested her to. Eventually, at Zeus' request, Hades did comply, but not before he made sure that Persephone dined with him. It was as a result of this that Demeter was forced to send back Persephone to the Underworld for one third of the year – the other two-thirds was the time she got to spend with her daughter – this was an eventual compromise that Zeus worked out. This myth served as the explanation of the ancient Greeks' explanation of winter. During these times, Demeter is said to be in mourning.

Artemis and Apollo

It is said that Artemis was the first of the twins to be born, and immediately after, she became a midwife in order to assist her mother in the delivery of her second child. Artemis went on to believe that the Fates had decided for her to be a midwife, because of the occurrence of this particular event.

Artemis and her vows

Artemis took her vows of chastity very deeply – and thus, requested her father Zeus to grant her the same: eternal virginity and chastity. She devoted her life to hunting, as well as to the protection of nature. There are some myths that say that Artemis lost her heart only to one individual, and that was her hunting partner, Orion. Still, she never broke her vows. All myths agree that Orion was eventually killed – but it remains unclear about whether it was Artemis, who was responsible, or Gaea, or Apollo.

Aphrodite and Hephaestus

As Aphrodite was widely regarded as the most beautiful goddess, Zeus was worried that there would be problems between other gods as they rivaled for her unparalleled attention. It was due to this reason that Zeus decided that she would marry Hephaestus, who was considered plain, and even the ugliest of the gods. The marriage between Aphrodite and Hephaestus was a forced one – and she was displeased by it, which caused her to have numerous other affairs, the most notable ones being those with Ares, and with Adonis.

Aphrodite, Adonis, and Persephone

Adonis was the grandson of the king of Cyprus, who was born after his mother, Myrrha, had been cursed by Aphrodite to feel lustful for her own father. Even though she was driven out and eventually changed into a myrrh tree, she gave birth to Adonis. Aphrodite took the baby to the Underworld, where Persephone fostered him.

When she returned and tried to claim him back after he had grown (and was known for his beauty), the two goddesses decided to let Zeus decide their fate. He decided that Adonis would have to split his year into three equal parts – one part he would have to spend with Persephone, one part he would have to spend with

Aphrodite, and he would be allowed to choose whom to spend the last one third with. Adonis chose Aphrodite, which allowed them to stay by each other for longer.

After his death at the hands of a wild boar, Aphrodite mourned over him, and let anemones grow wherever his blood was spilled. When Persephone welcomed Adonis' shade in the Underworld, a fight broke between the goddesses again. Yet again, Zeus had a role to play in the final decision – he stated that Adonis would spend half the year with Persephone, and the other half with Aphrodite.

Aphrodite, Ares, and Hephaestus

Like mentioned in the previous tale, Aphrodite's marriage to Hephaestus had not left her happy. For this reason, she looked for comfort in more than one partner – one of which was Ares. However, this affair did not stay hidden for too long, and Hephaestus found out about it through the Titan god, Helios – and decided to lay out a trap for them, for the next time they met.

When the two were together in bed, Hephaestus trapped them using a net that was unbreakable and so finely made it was almost invisible, and dragged the naked god and goddess to Mount Olympus, in order to make sure they felt ashamed. The other gods laughed at this sight, and it was Poseidon who eventually convinced Hephaestus to free them on the condition that Ares paid the fine of the adulterer.

The Titanomachy

So we have already read how Zeus rebelled against his father, Cronos, and made him regurgitate the rest of Zeus' siblings. It is not clear what happened immediately after this, but we know that the Titanomachy – a ten year long war between the gods and the Titans – began soon after. There was a poem by the same name, but it has been lost, and so has much information about the war with it.

While some of the second generation Titans like Menoetius fought alongside their family, some others like Prometheus and Epimetheus didn't do so. The war was fought without either side winning for a long time, and since all of them were immortals, there were no permanent casualties. The gods used Mount Olympus as their base, while the Titans used Mount Othrys as theirs. Towards the end though, the gods started winning with the help of older powers on their side.

During Uranus' reign, he had banished the Cyclopes and the Hecatoncheires (Hundred Handed Ones) to Tartarus. On Gaea's advice, Zeus liberated these beasts, and they helped him win the war. The Cyclopes were the ones who forged their godly weapons: Zeus' thunderbolt, Hades' helm of darkness, and Poseidon's trident. The Hecatoncheires helped by hurling a constant barrage of huge rocks at the Titans during the final battle. After the war, when many of the Titans were imprisoned in Tartarus, the Hecatoncheires became their jailors.

Prometheus and Epimetheus were not imprisoned, and neither were many of the female Titans, for they didn't participate in the war. Some of these Titans became the mothers of the Horai, the Muses, and other spirits. Atlas' punishment was one of the harshest. He was condemned to hold the weight of the sky (Uranus) on his shoulders for all eternity. Some later myths say that the Titans were eventually released from their punishment, even Cronos, who was instated as the ruler of the Isles of the Blest, the part of the underworld where the souls of brave heroes went.

The Olympians, however, didn't enjoy their peace for a long time. Gaea apparently got very furious with the gods, and wanted to punish them, so she created a monster called Typhon and sent him to destroy the gods. Typhon was a giant monster whose trunk crawled with dragon heads and whose nostrils shot flames. His screams were so terrifying that the gods fled from Olympus and transformed themselves into animals. Zeus later returned to fight Typhon, ashamed by his own cowardice, and, after a great struggle, emerged triumphant.

In another myth, Rhea, the wife of Cronos, released a deadly monster named Enceladus on the gods to avenge Typhon. He was defeated and chained under Mount Etna where his angry and painful cries were heard for a long time to come.

Gaea was not done yet. She encouraged her other sons, the Giants, to revolt against the Olympians and the overthrow the order created by them, which the Giants refused to acknowledge. Each of the Giants was a perfect match for an Olympian god, created solely to destroy their godly counterpart. The war between the gods and the Giants came to be known as the Gigantomachy, in which the Olympian gods, yet again, emerged victorious.

The Ages of Man

The 5 Ages of Man, from the "Golden Age" to the current "Iron Age", are described by Hesiod in his epic poem *Works and Days*. He was a farmer inspired by the Muses to write this 800-line poem describing the story of creation.

The Golden Age

The first period of man, according to Greek mythology, is referred to as the Golden Age. During this period, everything was joyful and easy, with mortals living like gods on earth, and dying easy deaths, as if falling asleep. There was no need to work, no one was ever sad, and springtime lasted forever. There was no evil, and every resource was available in abundance. It is even said that people aged in reverse during the Golden Age, becoming diamones and roaming the earth after their death. The Golden Age was the time when Cronos reigned, and it ended when Zeus defeated him.

The Silver Age

Zeus created the second generation of man during the Silver Age, inferior to the previous one in both form and intelligence. The year was divided by Zeus into four seasons: summer, spring, autumn, and winter. Man had to work, plant grains, and look for proper shelter. The comfort of the Golden Age was gone, but a child could still play for a hundred years before entering adulthood. After attaining adulthood, however, they only lived a short life, as described by Hesiod, spending their time in sorrow because of their inability to stay away from sinning and wronging each other. These people didn't honor the gods, and this enraged Zeus, who later destroyed them.

The Bronze Age

The Bronze Age was of strong and warlike men, fashioned from ash trees by Zeus. Hesiod mentions that all their equipment, their armor, their homes, and everything else was made of bronze. One notable thing about this race was that they didn't eat bread. They were described as terrible and strong, with tough skins and unconquerable arms. These men were adamant and strong of heart, and reveled in deeds of violence. It is said that they were destroyed by their own hands, and left nothing but the bright sunlight behind as they passed to the underworld.

The Heroic Age

The fourth period of man was the Heroic Age, just before our own time. Created by Zeus, the mortals of this age were known for their heroic deeds. They were more noble and righteous that both their successors and predecessors. Many of them were demigods who took part in the legendary Greek wars, and went to the underworld and the Isles of the Blest after their deaths, where they finally had honor and glory.

The Iron Age

The present race of men, the fifth one, was created by Zeus in what was referred to as the Iron Age by Hesiod. It is said that all sorts of evils materialized during this age, and all virtues which the gods prized so much in mortal men, started disappearing. Most of the gods abandoned this race, and even though there is some amount of good mingled with the evil in the present race, Zeus will end it when the time comes.

Chapter 5: Other Deities

There are countless other deities in the Greek mythology who are all recognized for the various roles they played, and they all have legends and folklore attached to them. Here, we shall take a look at some of them.

Asclepius

In ancient Greek mythology, Asclepius was known as the god of medicine, representing the 'healing' trait of medical arts. He wasn't always a god, as the legend goes, but was turned into one later, after his death.

Asclepius' mother, Coronis (also known as Arsinoe), was impregnated by the god Apollo, but later fell in love with a guy named Ischys. When Apollo came to know of this, he sent his sister, Artemis, to slay Coronis. It is said that as her body was burning on the funeral pyre, the white feathers of crows were forever stained black from the fumes. The baby Asclepius was delivered by Apollo himself during this time. Apollo later gave the child to Chiron, who raised him.

Chiron raised Asclepius to be the most talented doctor of that time, teaching him the art of surgery, the use of drugs, incantations, and much more. One version of the Trojan War story says that he also fought alongside the Achaeans, and cured Philoctetes of his snake bite by using Gorgon blood, which is said to have magical properties, capable of bringing the dead back to life when taken from the right side of a Gorgon. According to Homer's Iliad, however, this was done by Machaon or Podalirius, both of them Asclepius' sons.

Asclepius was believed to be so powerful that he could even resurrect the dead. This did not sit well with some, Zeus being one of them. He was especially enraged when he found out Asclepius had started accepting money for this. So he smote Asclepius with his thunderbolt. In one version of the story, he did so when Asclepius had resurrected Hippolytus at Athena's request. This incident is meant to show man's powerlessness to change the natural order of things. This is what separates mortals from gods.

Zeus later realized how important Asclepius was to the world of men, and decided to place him in the sky as a constellation named Ophiuchus, which means 'serpent-bender'. This is a reference to Asclepius' wand, which was entwined with a snake. This symbol went on to become a popular symbol for physicians of the modern world. It is sometimes confused with the Caduceus of Mercury, which has *two* intertwined snakes and a pair of wings. The Caduceus has been a symbol of commerce for a long time.

Asclepius fathered six daughters and three sons with his wife Salus (also called Epione). His daughters Hygieia, Meditrine and Panacea represent hygiene, medicine and healing power respectively, while sometimes his son Telesforos also symbolizes recovery.

Dione

In Homer's Iliad, Dione was primarily shown as Aphrodite's mother. She is sometimes seen as the female form of Zeus, her name being more of a title than a name: "The Goddess". Aphrodite has also been called Dionaea and Dione at times, and the Roman goddess Diana also has a similar etymology. Dione has been shown to be an equivalent of Gaea in some accounts, and she is also believed to have given birth to other children, the proof of which has been lost through time.

Dione's parentage is unclear. Sometimes, she is considered as a child of Gaea and Uranus. Other times, she is considered a daughter of the void. Some also consider her a daughter of the Titan Atlas, and some an Oceanid, Hesiod's Thogony being one of them.

Dione was the goddess who accompanied Zeus, not Hera, according to many votives inscriptions at the ancient Oracle of Dodona. Doves are considered Dione's dearly loved birds and priestesses, also called Pleiades. Dove is also the sacred bird of Dione's daughter, Aphrodite.

The Furies

Erinyes or Eumenides, in Greek mythology, were the female embodiments of retribution. They are popularly known by their Roman name, the Furies. The Erinyes were born from the blood of Uranus when it fell on the Earth as his son, Cronus, castrated him. But another account claims they came from Nyx. Their numbers are indeterminate; however three of them are widely recognized: Alecto, Megara, and Tisiphone. Their appearance has mostly been depicted as appalling and terrifying, with serpent-wreathed heads and blood-dripping eyes. They have also been shown to have bat-like wings or the body of a dog.

The Erinyes were believed to uphold the natural order of things, and persecute anyone who tried to break this natural order. Helios was once warned by Heraclitus about the wrath of the Erinyes in case he decided to change the course of the Sun. But they were mostly responsible for the persecution of mortals for breaking the natural law. They were especially brutal to those who committed patricide, fratricide, or involved themselves in other acts of familial killings.

When not on the lookout for victims on the Earth, the Furies were believed to dwell in Tartarus, where they tortured the damned souls of their victims. One popular example of their justice was the persecution of Orestes, who murdered his mother, Clytemnestra, because Apollo had instructed him to kill the murderer of his father, Agamemnon, which turned out to be his mother.

Through the ages, the Erinyes have been addressed by various names, some of which scholars believe to be euphemisms for their real name. Others just represent the terrible and punishing nature of the Erinyes. The Potniae (the Awful Ones), the Semnai (the Venerable Ones), the Maniae (the Madness), and the Dirae (the terrible) are some of their names.

Eris

Eris, also known as Discordia in Latin, was the goddess of chaos and discord in Greek mythology. She was a child of Zeus and Hera. She is the opposite of the Greek goddess Harmonia, also known as Concordia in Latin. She has been equated with Enyo (the goddess of war) by Homer. She was frequently seen as accompanying her brother Ares when he went to battles. She sows discord and chaos, and is mostly disliked and denigrated by other gods and mankind. She also brings her son Strife with her at times when she is riding in Ares' chariot.

Hebe

Hebe (Roman Juventas), was the Greek goddess of youth. Daughter of Hera and Zeus, she served as the cupbearer for the Olympian gods and goddesses, bringing their ambrosia and nectar. She also helped some of them in various chores, like preparing baths and helping them get in chariots. After being married off to Heracles, she was succeeded by Ganymede, the young prince of Troy. And this is why she is also sometimes referred to as "Ganymede".

The name Hebe came from the Greek word for "youth". Similarly, Juventas also means "youth". The word "juvenile" comes from it. Hebe was the one who granted

Iolaus his youth again so that he could fight Eurystheus. In Roman mythology, boys offered coins to Juventas when they entered adulthood. So in both the forms, she is primarily connected to youth or the prime time of life.

She is generally depicted donning a sleeveless dress. Antonio Canova's four statues of Hebe are famous, and they are placed in Italy's Museum of Forli. Hebe gave birth to two children, Alexiares and Anicetus, both fathered by Hercules.

Thanatos

Thanatos was the Greek god of death. The name itself means death, and in Greek mythology, he was shown as the personification of death. The Roman equivalent of Thanatos is the god Mors. Twin brother to Hypnos, the god of sleep, he was a son of Erebus and Nyx.

In earlier accounts, when death used to be regarded as a painful and sad moment, Thanatos was shown as a powerful figure with a fierce face and an unkempt beard, carrying a sword. His arrival was marked by gloom and agony. In later ages, however, he came to be perceived as an attractive young man. This was mostly because of the lucrative option of attaining Elysium after death. Roman sarcophagi often show him as a winged boy. Sometimes, he was also depicted as carrying a butterfly, meant to represent a soul. In some other accounts, he was shown as carrying an inverted torch or a wreath, and also having two wings attached to his belt at times.

In mythological accounts, Thanatos has sometimes been outwitted, most famously by Sisyphus, who accomplished it twice. The first time, he chained Thanatos in his own shackles, and hence, stopping any mortal from dying for a while. Thanatos was eventually rescued by Ares, who also handed Sisyphus to him, but the latter again persuaded Zeus into permitting him to return to his beloved, thereby cheating death again. Thanatos was also outwrestled by Heracles in the house of Admetus. After defeating Thanatos, Heracles was rewarded with the gift to have Alcestis revived.

Pan

In Greek mythology, Pan was considered the god of the wild, shepherds and goatherds, hunting, country music. He was also known to accompany nymphs sometimes. His name came from the ancient Greek word paein, which means "to pasture". In appearance, he was similar to a satyr (Roman faun), mostly human but with hindquarters and horns of a goat. He was also connected to fertility and spring season.

Although mostly considered to be a son of Hermes, Pan's parentage is still unclear. Some believed him to be a son of Zeus or Dionysus. In yet another myth, Pan's parents were Apollo and the mortal Penelope (Odysseus' wife). He was also equated with the Roman god Faunus. Pan was a lover of all things wild and regarded as an excellent musician, often depicted as a playful and joyous satyr dancing with nymphs. He was usually worshipped in wild places rather than in temples. His cult began from his place of birth, Arcadia.

Pan was also regarded as the creator of the musical instrument Syrinx. This is a famous myth, in which Syrinx was a beautiful water-nymph, daughter of the river god Landon. One day while returning from the hunt, she encountered Pan, and in order to avoid his compliments and insistencies, she ran away to Mount Lycaeum where her sisters turned her into a reed pipe so she could hide. The reeds produced mournful melodies when air was blown through them, and as Pan was still very much infatuated with her, he took some of those reeds, and cut them into seven (nine in some versions) pieces to form the Syrinx.

The word "panic" also comes from the name of Pan. There are several explanations for the origin of this word. In one version, Pan let out a terrifying cry during the Titanomachy (the war between Titans and

Olympians) that caused the Titans to flee, and he claimed credit for the victory of the Olympians. Another version states he used to scare the travelers going through the wild at night with his yelling.

Pan was also famous for his sexual powers. He was often depicted with a phallus, and was known to run after nymphs. He was also known to procreate with animals such as sheep and goats. This is where the word "pansexual" comes from. It is said that Pan learned to masturbate from his father Hermes, and later taught it to shepherds. His most famous sexual conquest was that of Selene, the moon goddess. He covered himself in sheepskin to hide his hairy body and drew the goddess down into the forest from the sky, and then seduced her.

Nemesis

Nemesis, also known as Rhamnusia and Adrasteia, was the Greek goddess of divine justice and revenge. She was regarded as a brutal and remorseless goddess, chiefly directing her anger towards those who were guilty of arrogance or Hubris, especially human arrogance towards gods and natural laws. She pursued the impudent ones with great vehemence, and exacted divine punishment. She is also known to curse those who had countless gifts, as she firmly believed nobody should have too much good.

Some believed her to be a daughter of Oceanus, while others like Hesiod claimed she was a daughter of Nyx and Erebus. Her name used to mean "just punishment for hubris" or "the distributor of what was deserved, neither good nor bad", but it has mostly lost that meaning now. In modern times, the term "nemesis" is generally used to refer to an archenemy or an unbeatable foe.

She often appears in literature and Greek tragedies, giving the protagonist what was due. When it comes to Nemesis, the myth of Narcissus is very popular. He was a handsome youth who was too arrogant for his own good. He harbored a disdain for anyone who loved him. This didn't sit right with Nemesis, and she led him to a pool. Legend has it that he fell in love with his own reflection and as a result, was unable to move from there. He died there eventually, and was later turned into a flower by Aphrodite, who was a lover of all things beautiful. The story of Narcissus is also where the word "narcissism" comes from.

Persephone

Persephone was the daughter of Demeter and Zeus, and the consort of Hades. She was also called Proserpine or

Proserpina by the Romans. Persephone was associated with springtime usually, and she was seen as an innocent maiden before she was abducted by Hades and became the queen of the Underworld. After that, the mortals became more fearful of her, and avoided saying her name, referring to her by titles such as "The Maiden" and "The Iron Queen". She became to be seen as cold and unforgiving.

In many myths, Persephone was also seen as just another aspect of the goddess Demeter, and not her daughter. Both of them were referred to as "Demeters", or "the goddesses". The story of her abduction carries great sentimental power, and is also the basis of how the Greeks explained the change of seasons.

BONUS CHAPTER: HORUS – Why the Egyptian God Matters

There are a lot of gods and goddesses in the world of mythology, but some of them are a little more obscure and forgotten than others. Horus, the Egyptian god of pretty much everything has a story to be told and it's significant into giving us insights into what ancient Egypt might have been like. So who was Horus? Why was he declared as the national god of ancient Egypt? Inside this book, you'll find answers to those and the role that this peculiar and interesting god played in the formation of basic Egyptian mythology.

Who the Heck is Horus?

Ancient Egyptians had a weird mythology. Honestly, if

you're looking for a definition of what Egyptians used to believe, it fits more along the lines of a death cult than pantheism. You see, the Egyptians were obsessed with death. It hung over them like the molten sun that bakes down on the Nile and the Sahara desert. Not only did they have one of the oldest civilizations in the world, but they are also one of the most mysterious. Clouded with superstition, confusion, and mysticism, Egyptian gods and goddesses have been reduced to cartoon icons that we really don't know much about.

So who the heck was Horus?

When I say Horus, those of us who are fairly well versed in mythology will probably identify him as the dude with a hawk's head. Fair enough, but he went way beyond having just a hawk's head.

Egyptians believed that when the Pharaoh was alive, that he was actually the embodiment of Horus. In death, it was believed that the Pharaoh became Osiris, but more about Osiris in another book. Right now, all we care about is Horus who actually holds the title of Egypt's first national deity. Though he went by many names, Horus retains a title of having significance in the Egyptian society way back when the pyramids were just a distant thought. As one of the major gods of ancient Egypt, he's worth knowing.

So why do we hear so little about guys like Horus? Well, that's because we're fairly permeated with Greco-Roman mythology in our public schools and Egyptian mythology is sort of a footnote in most of our textbooks. Think about it, how much did you actually read about ancient Egypt in your school classes? The most significant thing that we all know about ancient Egypt is that they built the pyramids and that pretty much sums it up.

The goal of this book is to help rectify that a little for you. Who the heck was Horus? Well, he was a complex god of great significance to the people who worshipped him and has had the great misfortune of being forgotten in the current time period. So how about we spread a little more knowledge of this god and have spread the word about him.

Let's dive right in.

In the Beginning

The best place to start is always at the beginning. For Horus, he does not have the distinction of being an omnipresent deity, but rather has a definite genesis in the Egyptian mythology. This means that he was born between the union of another god and goddess. This makes him a third generation deity and much like the

Grecian religion; he's still on par with his forefathers.

The most common myth of Horus' birth is that he is the product of the union of the god Osiris and the goddess Isis. In order to understand just how Isis and Osiris got together, you're going to need a little back story which is seriously intense, so strap in.

So, Osiris is the king of the gods and held sway over the dominion of the gods and was the brother of Set who was the god of war, chaos, and the desert. Naturally, when you're the god of basically all bad things, you envy the popularity and the power of those who have it better off than you and Osiris had it way better off. After all, he was married to his sister Isis. Now, Isis is considered the hottie with a really great body in the Egyptian pantheon and is so beloved that the Romans accepted her as a goddess in their own pantheon. So Osiris and Isis are happily married, doing divine stuff, when one night Set decides that he's going to take Osiris' throne and make it his own. But, in order to do that, he needs to get rid of Osiris permanently and that means killing him and sending his soul, or Ba, to the land of the dead.

Stumbling across Osiris sleeping, Set is overcome with complete and utter jealousy and kills his brother. But, remember that ancient Egypt is basically a very large, very organized death cult. So they believed greatly in resurrection and the afterlife. Fearing that someone would find a way to bring Osiris back from the land of the dead, Set took out his handy axe and started hacking Osiris into fourteen pieces and scattered his body parts far and wide. Not only is Set a kin-slaying psychopath, but he's also kind of a dick. With Osiris' body dismembered and spread far and wide, Set ascends the throne and becomes king of everything.

The end.

Not if Isis had anything to do with it. Channeling her feminist: "I don't need a man's help" side, Isis sets out on an epic quest to acquire all fourteen pieces of her husband's body. So in love with him, she eventually finds all of his body parts and reassembles him, embalms him, and does the traditional mummy stuff needed to give his soul rest in the afterlife. Well, once Osiris is completely intact, Isis decides that it's time for one last ride with her husband, for old times' sake.

Cue the necrophilia.

So after he's dead, Osiris gets Isis pregnant and suddenly returns to "life" only this time he's a living corpse and now reigns supreme over the land of the dead and the souls of the just. Filled with anger at Set, he realizes that there's not much he can do from the great beyond and looks to his wife's swollen belly. Boom, thus Horus is born and he's here to kick some serious butt...

The God of... Disturbing Behavior

Before we continue with the Osiris myth, it's important that you understand that the Osiris myth is foundational and offers fundamental insights into the Egyptian faith. Notice the importance and the manipulation of death. Osiris is killed, but through the proper rituals, he is brought back to life in a sense. In fact, he becomes the ruler of this land beyond life and the idea of a paradisal afterlife is very appealing to the Egyptians.

As for Horus, he represented the living aspects of his father. In the times to come, Horus became the icon of the living Pharaohs, the symbol of a living god. In a sense, he was the national god or the god of leadership and the kingdoms, particularly Upper Egypt. However, Horus eventually took the mantle of the United Kingdom as well. So not only is he the symbol of Egypt, he is also the God of the Sky which we'll talk about later. The sky was of huge importance to the Egyptians and eventually led to the fusion of the gods Ra and Horus, but again, I'll talk about that later. But finally, Horus was seen as the god of war and hunting and here's why.

Because he vowed to take back his father's throne.

So Horus was born and Isis and Osiris pretty much told him that Set stole his place and that the gods were fairly helpless to dethrone Set, nor were they particularly interested in doing so. The other gods had their own concerns and the ruler of Egypt/the World didn't really bother them. They basically told Horus to figure it out himself.

What follows is a series of battles that left both of them helpless and exhausted from warring against each other. So when the other gods took notice of this perpetual war, they told the gods to figure out who was ruler and to do it fast because the war was ravaging the world. After an awesome war, what follows is kind of disturbing and downright weird.

They decide to sexually assault each other. Yup, it became a war to see who could get their semen inside the other. The first one to get some sperm inside the other would be declared superior and the ruler of Egypt. So, Set disguises himself as a super hot woman and approaches Horus and starts to seduce him. When they decide to get down and dirty, Horus finally realizes that Set's a dude and sticks his hand between Set's legs and catches his stuff before it can get inside him. I have a hard time picturing how a bird headed man was getting raped by an aardvark like creature disguising itself as a hermaphroditic woman, but that's what went down. Horus caught his junk and threw it into the river.

Well, the gloves were off and Horus was pissed by what just went down. He went to find Set's favorite food, which turned out to be lettuce. Getting his stuff all over the leaves, he skipped off into the night and watched as Set gobbled down his favorite snack without knowing.

So the two went to the gods who would pass judgment and see who would be declared king after successfully sexually assaulting the other. The gods called out to Set's sperm and it slithered up out of the river and answered them. Upon seeing this, the gods declared that Set had failed. When they called out to Horus' sperm next, Set's stomach rumbled and thus ended the century long war of who was the rightful ruler and who was sexually disturbed for the rest of eternity.

Thus, Horus became the King of Egypt.

One Last Fight

Angry that Horus had beaten him in the battle of sexually assaulting one another, Set wanted one last chance to win the throne of Egypt. Agreeing that there should be one last challenge so that there is no question whatsoever that Horus was the better being, Horus obliged set. The gods, completely and utterly exhausted by all of this, said that they could do whatever they wanted, just that it ended after this competition. So the rules were set down.

They were to have a boat race on the Nile River with boats made out of stone. Whoever won the race would finally, once and for all, from that moment to the end of time, be declared king and ruler of Egypt. Clearly neither of them understood a thing about stone or water.

Except, Horus did it. Now, before we go any farther, Set is known as a Trickster deity. Practically all pantheons have a deity that is renowned and infamous for their pranks, tricks, and mischief. Surprisingly, for Egypt, it wasn't Horus, even though he's clearly well versed in shady tactics. It's actually Set who is known as the Trickster Deity and what happens is beyond understanding, but Horus once again outsmarts the Trickster.

Before the day of the big race, Horus cuts down a whole bunch of trees and crafts a magnificent boat out of wood and tests to make sure that it's perfect and that it'll float. All the while, Set is acting like an idiot carving his own boat out of beautiful stone that's fit for a god and the future King of Egypt. But, before Horus is done with his boat, he paints it so that it looks like stone and presents it to the gods on the day of the race. Looking it over, they decide that it's made of stone and that it's totally ready for this race. Set's boat is also declared to be made out of stone and the conditions of the race are met.

Now, the race goes off exactly like you'd expect. Horus' "magic" boat floats like a freaking miracle and he drifts off down the Nile with a grin on his face. Set, on the other hand, drops his boat into the water and is strangely baffled by the fact that it sinks, like a rock in the water. Horus is declared the winner and Set willingly offers the role of Egypt's true leader to Horus. He never once questions Horus' boat or tactics. Instead, he goes out into the deserts and wastes and plants his flag, calling this his new home.

Instead, Horus sets up shop and is declared the ruler of Egypt forever.

What Horus Teaches Us

As far as myths go, there's a lot that can be learned about Egypt's moral compass and code during their ancient civilization. As their supreme god when it comes to the living, Horus has a lot to teach us about ancient Egypt and I'm going to give you some things you can take away from Horus.

The first thing is that war is a divine accord. War is not something that is necessary, but it's an entity that has been commissioned and enacted by the gods. If the gods go to war, then why would people question the existence of war? This is significant because whenever war came up, an easy way to rally the masses was to cite Horus. Oh and did I mention that Set was the figurative god of foreigners too? Horus was a war icon and a figure that Pharaohs and heads of state could conjure up whenever war was on the horizon and the masses flocked to bring honor to their god and to channel him.

The justification of underhanded tactics! When Horus does something that is super shady and quite frankly evil, it's seen as cunning and smart. This is a way to publicly justify doing what needs to be done, no matter the cost or the road that is required to be traveled. This also comes into play when Horus merges with Ra because Horus believes that he is entitled to the power of the solar god as well. Horus' behavior is often appalling, but he is also seen as divinely gifted in behaving such. This means that there was no questioning the Pharaoh's actions. If they did something horrifying or appalling, then who are the people to question the living manifestation of Horus?

The necessity of unity for Egypt! For those of you that know something about the history of Egypt, you know that it was in a constant state of civil war between the Upper Kingdom and the Lower Kingdom. The legends of Horus are symbolic of the subjugation of the Lower Kingdom that led to the unity that gave Egypt some of its greatest moments of stability, expansion, and power. The struggle of Set and Horus bring into the minds of the masses the necessity of Egypt being one. Horus is the icon of their power, their strength, and their cunning when it comes to facing outsiders of threats within.

Horus is a strange god, but most pantheon gods have their dark streak and he's no exception. However, Horus is seen as a heroic figure and is often called upon by those who are in their hour of need. For those living in ancient Egypt, Horus was more than a strange legend, but rather an icon that all of Egypt could rally behind and stand strong with. So next time you find yourself in a position where you need to talk about some mythological being, think about reminding people around of who Horus was. He's got a tale or two that are pretty interesting.

Conclusion

With this, we come to the end of the book – which sadly means it is time for us to step back into reality.

I have attempted to give you an overview of the Greek gods – and presented them according to different generations of deities that they formed. Through that, attempted to present you with tales about some of the gods, which we hope made for an interesting read. However, you must remember that the tales about different gods and goddesses in Greek mythology as far from restricted to just this book – there are so many more stories, that looking them up can be quite a daunting task!

I hope that this book rekindled your interest in Greek mythology and sparked an interest in you to help you find out even more. Greek mythology has many more stories to offer – such as the ones involving heroes, and the different creatures in ancient Greece, and even the monsters – the list is far from exhaustive!

As with any mythology that is native to a place, the stories in Greek mythology show us how ancient Greeks attempted to understand and explain the occurrences in the world. That makes it even more interesting.

I hope that this journey you made, to ancient Greece and back, proved to be an interesting one.

You May Enjoy Roy's Other Books

Greek Mythology: Guide to Ancient Greece, Titans, Greek Gods, Zeus and More!

Hyperurl.co/greekmyths

Egypt: Egyptian Mythology and the Secrets of the Gods

Hyperurl.co/Egypt

Greek Mythology: Myths and Legends of the Gods, Titans, Zeus, Olympians and More!

Hyperurl.co/greekmyths

Viking Mythology: Ancient Myths, Gods and Warriors

Hyperurl.co/Viking